RHIME of TIME

PADMAJA
BHARTI

BlueRose
Publishers

First Published in August 2020

ISBN: 978-93-90380-25-1

BLUEROSE PUBLISHERS

www.bluerosepublishers.com

info@bluerosepublishers.com

+91 8882 898 898

Cover Design:

Varij Vinayak

Typographic Design:

Tanya Raj Upadhyay

Distributed by: BlueRose, Amazon, Flipkart, Shopclues

Preface

This book *Rhime Of Time* dedicated to my mother, Mrs. Meena Rani Das, and my father, Mr. Gopal Das, for their constant support and motivation throughout my life and in this book. My Dad, though not a writer, has always inspired me to read a lot. Reading and writing have become a habit now because of him.

The majority of my writings in this book inspired by the beauty of mother nature/ Mahadev Shiva/ Durga ji/ Sun God/ Love and Human behavior/nature.

If you observe, you will find several deep meanings in all of my poetry. I tried to connect and compare mother nature with human nature. I do try rhymed poetry, and few are blank verses. I can say this book has both types of writings- old style and modern too. I used new words and phrases to make this book more interesting to read. I am extremely inspired by freewriting, though my poetries are part of automatic writing.

You can read motivational poetries in detail and also just in two lines like:

"*You Are Your Sun.... When You Arise....*
Your Sun Will Shine.... On Your Brighter Side...."

I believe writing has power and can inspire life.

"*Pen Is A Weapon.... Without Need for Red Ink....*
It's Dancing in My Hand and Expressing It's Feelings...."

\- ***Padmaja Bharti***

SPECIALLY DEDICATED TO TEACHERS

"TEACHING TO STOP LIFE SUFFERING"

New Age College-Going Kid

Here I am going to describe the role of teachers in a student's life both during college and post-college life and how the teachers can influence, guide, and mould the life of a student for a better tomorrow.

"NEW AGE COLLEGE-GOING KID"

"Right to having a creepy crap,
Most of us will keep the craps,
Not even in single die;
We are dying all our hap..."
"Just to have better attire,
The cost of living is not even a single snap..."

The above poetry is an explanation of the emotions of a new age college-going kid. Whether they want to or not, they have to face some non-sense from the surrounding environment, and most of them will keep the non-sense inside their head, which develops a 'fire' inside. This fire is not letting them up in their life. They are frustrated and dying inside.

All these golden days where they need to be happy spent dying, as their happiness inside their head is dying. Because all of us want to show our good nature, not the fire inside our brains, to live lives uncomplicated, college-goers cannot keep a single good memory during college days. Because of ragging and their bad experiences, especially during the first year with college mates, they might suffer their whole life with bad experiences.

A Window For The World

"TEACH THE TEACHER"

"Teach the Teacher without means...
The real-life Teacher is your glimpse...
Gazing your glimpse teaches you all your means...
And life will be full of rimes...

Here in the above poetry, I want to tell the teachers, to teach such a lesson that will not only give meaning but also teach about the satisfaction in life, about how to be incredible without being kind, and teachers should tell them that there is something inside of you that is wonderful and that is your real-life Teacher, who is going to help you all the time (That is your inner power).

Just that wonderful "You" should not die, and you have to keep your eyes open for your wonders. In this way, life will be poetic and beautiful.

"NEVER WIPE OUT YOUR DUSTY NATURE"

"Never wipe out your dusty nature...
It may have you and your bold character...
The College will give you just a passion...
You have to develop Art out of passion..."

Above poetry is saying not to be too much goody to all of us. Despite having a lousy sight, we can always comprise it for being helpful. Just let it go. Your bold character can make you survive in this mixed world. College can only give you just your zeal and passion, but you have to use it well to develop an ideal living with your zeal and create an Art out of desire.

"CAMOUFLAGE"

"Camouflage being is all your Art of living...
But having ahead of the lion can't let you expire..."

Is the above lines are about living and being. It conveys that teachers should teach how to become famous and unpopular at the same time. Teachers also should explain how to improve good habits and keep the bad one sat bay. You don't need to be like a lion always. Sometimes, accordingly, you have to camouflage and mix with everyone.

"COLLEGE FINISHED"

"College finished...Life is giggling...
Not to worry...If you are suffering...
Have a substance...To meet your back...
Strict bloom...All you need to find the rules..."

The above poetry covey shows a teacher is calling the student to meet them again. If College is over, then life may not be so easy to live. But you have to become keen to have a substance to meet your back. The Teacher is also saying to students; if you follow the rules strictly, you may happily bloom in your life.

"DON'T HAVE MULTIPLE DREAMS"

"Don't have many dreams...
Just have a single wink..."

In the above lines, Teacher is saying to the student to develop a passion at a time. Because having multiple emotions simultaneously is suitable for well-settled people, we initially have to concentrate on a single dream or a desire. You may be able to pursue passions, but you have to make a unique garland out of multiple emotions to complete it beautifully.

"TIME"

College race was just for the time being...
Life is waste if time will be innings..."

In the above poetry, the Teacher wants to tell the students that they don't just think of having a few days in the College. There's a new world waiting outside for you. As a life teacher (Time), College days can teach you a lot. Don't just think of the race. Think of living well and surviving well. Because once the time moves, you will be nothing. Without time, there is no world. So keep the time on your side. And keep moving without being a part of the race inside.

"COME ON TEACHER"

"Come on, Teacher...
Teach me the lesson...
With full of bloom...
Cost you nothing...
Just have a broom..."

Here, in this poetry, Students want to tell the Teacher to have beautiful teaching and also encourage the students to bloom in their life. And it is not going to cost you anything. Just take a broom and wash out negativity from our brains. This helps us to survive in this nasty world and bloom with full positiveness.

"CARE for YOURSELF"

"Care for yourself...
With the most sensational ...
Life has meaning...
Without being seasonal..."

In this above poetry, Teacher wants to tell the students, "You have to think twice and become more sensitive person inside, and care for it." And in the second sentence, Teacher is telling to students, "Life has meaning without being seasonal", which means "You have to be strong enough and run, walk, always crawl in life". Don't tell yourself that you are becoming lazy. You need to work hard always. And not from time to time.

"CORPORATE WORLD"

"Corporate World has no meaning...
Without having a steep rate..."

In the above lines, after coming to the corporate world, the Teacher is telling the students to become healthy and passionate. And, most importantly, challenging for the world to survive. The Teacher is saying that the corporate world is not going to see from inside. It will make you a difficult person that you have to become quiet inside.

Padmaja Bharti writes poems

In this book, she has written a few verses, she is describing herself in some complex and simple words as together in her poetry.

As a writer, she believes that writing has two criteria, and that is Costume and Attire. One is for living, and the other is to be free.

For her, writing is a medium for self-satisfaction, and that is simply attire.

Table of Contents

Mulberry

Listen….
My heart is speaking to you, my darling Mulberry….

Listen….
My Soul has found you too emotionally….

Your body carries your brain and sweet memories….
Your brain has the power to purify your unwanted pests,
so be carefree….

When the body of Silkworm became Cocoon and said….
I have the power to create silky tone luxury….

Description

Here poet wants to connect nature with our body and brain and suggesting to have a carefree life.

Gypsy

Life is a beautiful heart of the Gypsy girl....
She owes dreams and tried to fulfill....
But never forget about her inner self....

She moves all the circles around and finally got nothing to do....
She forgives her dreams and sleeps forever....
Do her senses kill her?

Match your senses with a gypsy heart....
Be gypsy by heart, but don't lose apart....

Say no to smoke and create a trend for the past, future, and present....
Be gypsy by heart but say no to grass....

Description

Here, the poet wants to say no to smoke & drugs. Criticized by the fact of unhealthy behavior.
The result shows the truth about smoking kills, perhaps being gypsy by heart will create an emotional connection between you and yourself.
So, Stay Happy and Don't Smoke.

Geometry Vs. Life

Sign of "Cross" signified and "Dot" classified….

The "Cross" means inwards or away from you….
The "Dot" means outwards or coming towards you….

The "Cross" has been signified all over the World as hope….
And the "Dot" has been classified as observing, and all is going fine….

When the "Cross" combines with the "Dot" like in 'Swastika'….
Hope and observing will step by our side….

Description

This poem describes the reality of history, where "Cross" and "Dot" has been used to form peace & harmony.

Demane!

Feel the pain….
Conquering own brain….
Flight and find real umbra….
The shadow will intern you….
Like a circle of dark demane!

Description

'Demane' is a Latin word that means 'Percolate' (to move gradually through a surface with tiny holes or spaces in it).

The whole meaning of this poem is, feel your pain or someone else is feeling the pain by conquering your brain.

Take a flight and find the real umbra (here 'Umbra' means an utterly dark area on the Earth caused by the Moon).

Why I have used this word is because, after conquering the brain, you will feel finding deep inside you as a hollow person. There is often chaos and turmoil, and that creates a shadow over your brain.

That shadow will pass inside you like the same circle of darkness demane (or moves slowly through you) now it's moving deep and more rooted in your body, brain, or heart.

Child Labor

Hold that hand….

Mold it on....

Make it your brand....

So that, with pride, she can pay for every bite she takes....

The child is like clay....
Please don't slay....

Description

We can mold a child's brain like clay, because when they are small, it's moldable and how we how, that's important.

Love On Fire

Deep inside, Love is rising with the fire and making cloud fading in droplets of water....

The iced cold of this lovely lady moor....
Blooming with these fading droplets....
When it is touching her endure....
All in the fire of her cloudy attire and Love of desire....

Description

This poem describes extra-terrestrial activities, here moor is the Earth, and it's blooming when rains

And the poet is connecting it with Love.

Water Changes

Water can destroy fire….
But people say the fire has all the powers….

Having any other means of making them feel alike….
But when you want to destroy water….
It will evaporate and change its attire….
Fire can't destroy water….

Similarly, the human body can be buried or burned….
But the Soul can't be destroyed….

Description

The Soul is immortal.

Knowledge

Knowing is the best investment....

As greater the output....

As greater the input....

With interest....

Positive You

Life with wheel chair….
Caged bird with feathery fair….
Everything will be defined with time….

Have faith in your inner mind….
See negativity turns into positivity….

Like Daylight comes after every night….

No Suffering At All

Dated back to old covered book….
Full of dust within some hope….

Why is this book not telling me….
The story of first lady proof….

No name, No fame….
Nothing is curious about her….

In Jesus' last supper meal….
She was bond to be available….
What was her name…?
Mary Magdalene…!

Description

This poem describes how a lady lost her name and still have no suffering at all.

Choosing your book is as simple as choosing your inner God.

Peace of Mind

The day when I am close to Ocean….
Swimming deep is my favorite play….

In each stroke trying to swim deep inside the Soul of water….
I'm meeting to myself toxic inside….

Nobody trusted her back in the time….
Those toxins dilute whenever I see the deep ocean flowing into my mind….

Deep and more rooted in this ocean flowing through my eyes….
Finally, I touched the ground with full darkness all around but my search of Soul is founded now….
Which was having the blooming heart….

Found the pearl full white shinning like a star in this dark blue sky….

Description

The poem describes how to find our Soul through Love of nature.

In Search Of

Gold mine full of carbon inside....
Create folds in their path beside....

Where we search for the golden heart inside....

Description

The poem describes the search of precious and over-refined things that we need to go through, and the poet trying to imagine gold with the golden heart here.

Fighting Continues

Royalty comes with titles….
Birthmarks connect to identity….
Both have a sense of witty humor….

One is for the bride….
And the other is for right….

This is the fight….
All for being elite….

Description

The poem describes how this society moves with titles and identities. For being an aristocrat and false show off.

Truth of Life

The costume has the character….
You built in your mind so ever….

You keep the drama….
Own the makeup….

Cold-hearted you, fit in the costume….
You made it for never….
And have a life with imaginable caricatures….

Description

The poem describes each person in this World come with different character and costume (Body).

If you want to fit in this World, you have to be cold-hearted to fit in. And you had this life with myths.

Searching Life

We should earn for life….
Not earn to live….

The happy life is such a myth….
Earning money is all to switch….

Description

The poem describes how people are running for money without seeing that money and happiness as all myth.

Prickling Heat

Sprinkle of mine….
Welcoming the shine….

Grayish shade and growing shadow….
Prickling my heart and twinkling with rimes….

It's new to me….
Hoping all fine….

Description

The poem describes the poet, how she accepts all with mature shades, and growing outlines with excitement in her heart is a new person; she is expecting everything will be fine now.

Art of The Sunset

Night moon follows him on the gloom....
Undressed Moon in front of sunny groom....

Captured smile....
Tracing the shine....

Holding Hands....
In evening bright....

Is this night shape them inside...?
Or separate apart...!

Description

Here the poet is describing Sunset beauty like a love story between the Sun and the Moon.

In Full Moon Street

Crowded street....
Full of flowers and sweets....

One whom I loved, called me nasty in public succeed....
Love has no boundaries....
But I'm quite....

Still in this flourish street....
Catch me if you can, in your dream....

The smell of me can't reach you....
As costly flowers in this pricey street....

I'm pricey....
Flourishing and jazzy....
In this full moon street....

Description

The poem describes her love failure. But the poet is flourishing and becoming a social person now.

Let's Go

Let's Go….
Going to my way, be in the war….
And flourish, they flaw….

Let's Go….
Let's go to a beach and find white pearls among the sand and stones….

Sand is flowing like time….
And the stone is tough as my mind….
Let's go; this is the right time….

Let's go….
Let's go together till the end of my time….
Don't drop me in the middle and that might be end of my time….

When I am close to the limit, our time will tell you about being in infinite….
That's the reality of letting go in time….
You will become tough for being mine….

Let's go….
Let's go to find peace….
Away from all noise….
Let's take me to a busy market….

Though noise, there's no disturbance, and we can find peace…

Let's go….
Peace is coming with her smile….
All flow is in our mind….

We have to be in time to collect the memories and flourish and the shine….
Let's go….

Will

Though the path seems slippery….
My will of desire create my fine in history….

Having the noise inside my brain….
Will become the poetry….

The brain will solve the mysterious attire of my fire….
Will is solving my closed eye victory….
Solving my dreams of desire for amity….
Marvelous will is rewriting my own story….

Description

Here the poet wants to describe her inside and outside the World. Both are important, and her will is full of desire.

The Face

The face you have colored with guilt….

Nowadays, I am binding to cover her feelings….

I have chosen the best color in black script….

Description

Here, the poem describes a face that has been into so much pain and guilt and this guilt created by someone else.

And now the poet is trying to cover this face of feeling.

'The poet has chosen black script' means she is hiding it by writing.

Lust & Love

The heart is asking….
Don't you know about Lust & Love….

You are melting down totally on your feet….
Restless and crazy with your smell….

Fire inside burning sensation….
Holding on your skin….

How to be free from my heart's ownership….
Lusting love is my sin….

With you, I'm not with my mind….
Only the heart's ownership….

All My Thoughts

Moon street glazed with dual thoughts….
Something like pink or something like green….

Stars on the earthy ground….
Something like pink or something like green….

I'm feeling dreamy with my colors of thought….
Something like pink or something like green….

My imagination is growing like all psychedelic….
All colors smoky and frizzy….
She was coloring me as dizzier….

Water on my feet loving those reasons behind this lovely street….
All my thoughts….
All my thoughts….

Hippy Look

Popular early 1970s fashions women….

Look in my fashion….

I'm a woman of colors….

My smoky smiling red lips, touching your soft lyrics….

I'm singing the song of winnable, music addiction and romance, have to be….

In White

In White….
One bright blue moon night….
So quite….
Whispering your words….
It makes me feel like the Love Goddess Venus….

No lighting….
At all….
But you are feeling me like the Apollo God….

Sweet fight….
Continue with you….

Whole Night….
It is like a mesmerizing shower with sweat in your arms….

Description

Here the poet is describing divine lovemaking.

Black & White

What to write....
Making some sight....
In Black & White....

Colorful dreams....
Where Love bounded with her smile....

Opened her eyes....
And found the World in Black & White....

Never create duplicity in your own words....
Make it dark or bright....

Description

Here the poet is describing her writing how she bonded with her emotion. We shouldn't have duplicity in our character or in our words. Either it's colorful or Black & White.

A Step

The journey towards thousand miles....
Finding the meaning of life....

Life came and told me confined....
Every day take a small step....
Towards your goal....

It's equivalent to ....
Hundreds of in vain....

Vintage Mom

Those puffy sleeves….
Those nostalgic clips….
Reminding me my Mom's olden days pics….

Those gracious beauties as beautiful like charice dreams….
Reminding me of my Mother's saree with no border and rosy prints….

Those golden beauties and olden grace….
Reminding me of my Mom's straight hair soft and silk….

In her Love, In her dreams….
Those old days are all covered with fledging….

Skin Deep

Adoring my beauty mist….
Alluring and foggy kissed….

Sweet memories are having some thoughtfulness….
Never regret your make in effort….

Dropping Soul in your desire….
But beauty in only skin deep….

Keep biting your nails….
As deep ship sails….

Opening Eyes

An eye meant to be shy….
That shy is cold and mine….

Shining shy opening the door of eyes….

Lost in those eyes asking me….
Why you are having no fear….
To become cold and dry….

Shy, shining eyes saying loud and define….
I am yours….
And You are mine….

Serendipity

Waiting for the best evening….
When the Sun meets the Moon….

I was crossing the same street….
When fire having the bloom….

Revolving chair in my room….
Asking me to go back in my blues….

She was scratching the wound, Against the circle of doom….
Waiting for the time of serendipity by scratching my sweet wound….

Fish Soul

Deepwater fish has its desire of lust….
When do you see them, finding water with trust…?

Life of fish will have no sink….
Sinking inside is their smiley dreams….

When we compare, we too have the same but clitic aside….

Sound, its funny….
But we don't need money….

If we get alike, life is full of placid….
Like a fish swimming in our deep Soul inside….

School Days

My 7th-grade emotions….

Things were so unreal….
But one thing was real….

That was my creation….
Handwriting, deep calligraphy of words….
And symbolization of zest….

I never played in deep colours….
All I played was with shallow calligraphic emotions….

Zest was my sweet sense….
And conceptualization of Love….
Was little great emotion….

Life WithColours

Life with colors dipped in green….
Smoothie touches solving heart seems….

You are testing your feelings with smoky green….
Fencing your sound in and out….

Mind touches the ground of your smoky green….
Life with colors touches you deep….

My Solister

Deeper and deeper, you kissed my heart….
Find me when you missed my heart….

I am your Soul….
You are my Solister….

Glass With Substance

Empty glass is now saying….
A glass with "Substance of being broken" ….

Fill it once more….
To break it again….
With the warm water….
So that there will be no voice of pain….

Break it inside….
Again, and again….
Until there will be no emptiness again….

Make It Together

My wristwatch is flying like a kite….
Come and hold it, just for glide….

Rusted, twisted, come and make it beautified….
Follow me as I follow my flight….

Make it together….
Can create thundering nights….

Cooling, buzzing, fairy nights….
You are sinking us together in some sparkling light….

Clingy Thoughts

Clingy thoughts….
Curbing me inside….

Common flaws….
All in my mind….

Forming me in a frame….
Worth of a thousand words….

Holding me from my back….
Soft and lite….

Love of Mine

"Love of Mine" ….
You have been reminded….

Can't solve the mystery behind….
It's been diluted….

Knife to the heart….
He was cutting me apart….

Still, not missing you from inside….
Like a reward….

Books & Feelings

Books are kind of greeting me….
Cold wave pleasing me….

This is Love….
Hunching me….

No one can make….
Dazing me….

A Glowing Star

Draw the line at its end….
You will find yourself to get infinite….

Around the line….
Never-ending time….

Time is showing….
Secret line of infinite….

Curving around us….
And says not to define….

It's good or evil….
Because all white and black became one….

A glowing star….
Like the Sun….

One Day

Feelings will go one day….
Fingertips will slay one day….

Your touch will have a flaw one day….
Bezel sound will have crackling noise one day….

I am glowing inside….
That's killing me right this day….

My current town….
None is around this day….
Where is your noun this day…?

Feeling To Bloom

We have feelings….
But our nature having cult to devote….

We can't express our moony dealings….
Until our nature will die in high road….

Once in a blue moon….
Our feeling gets separated from our nature….
And that only can create a bloom….

Being Innocent

Going to bed with my own words....
Often means that nature is telling me....

This story was thinking about....
How to make a living with my desire....
How to remember this life is going to end up....

With being innocent....
In my Soul, divine....

Through my own words....
Makes it dark and fine....

Bronze Skin

Blackish will….
Whitish zeal….

Brownish fame….
And right here, I am the palette of smoky smiles….

My favorite color is dark bronze skin….

Single Snap

Right to having a creepy crap….
Most of us will keep the craps….

Not even in single die….
We are dying all our hap….

Just to have a better attire….
The cost of living is not even a single snap….

Love Lyrics

Will to make it more difficult....
My dreams...
Could you please hold my microphone...?

Just let me read....
The last sentence for you....

I have a simple dream....
Don't let it grow....
More than you....
My love lyrics....

As Always

Crossing your fingertips….
Touching the morning meeps….

And making all your caring natural feelings….
In my lips….
In my heart…
Of gypsy clips….

Collecting pictures….
Of my dreams….

Musical style….
In my wearing fairy tales….

Have me in your eyes….
As always….
As always….

Old Date

Coldwater stays on your feet….
Lives a happy life as you dreamed….

When you're ready for your clues….
Outside your home makes you feel good about your Soul….

Natural hair makes you feel better….
Shines me on your skin….

With you and your body feelings….
Making out not all your dreams….

For you and your body scent….
Now makes you want your care….

Dreams of your heart….
As you are outside, yourself….

Nice me….
Going back for years old date….

Volver

I will see you at....
On that side....

Never been in this World....
Even more than your hive....

Think like that Volver....
On your gentle side....

Back In Time

During this period of time….
My mind is sharing just vibes within our guideline….

Greater we fall….
Gradually it's winning time to go back….
And collect the nature of our sin….

Eternal Love

Today....
The Moon has the shape of You....

My eternal Love....

You are seeing me from the window....
Trance of you not letting me close my eyes....
The rest of me is your desire....

Aura

Writing needs more me....
Palm says you exist in my life....

God bless you....
And give you my all Sunshine....

Dreams have some sense....
And realize the reality....

Golden glimpse holds my hand....
Now you were the power of aura.

Twinkling Heart

Carbon blueprint was my attire....
Taken off my last attire....

Draw me in such a costume, never seen....
Such goodness in me by all means....

Drawing will bring my heart twinkling....
As always shown by me....

Zeal

My heart is mediating with my Soul….

Lustrous World entering my will….

Dewdrop shines in the morning light….

I want to hear signing birds' zeal….

Words of World

World of relations....
Physical is not bond with Mental....

Words of World....
Can touch the sound....
Both Physical & Mental....

The connection has been broken by lost cult....
The reason behind every moment....
Has to bond with words of World....

With Me or Without Me

Block me….
From Yourself….

Right or Wrong….
All your desire….

Killing me….
Inside the fire….

In this World….
Being your slave….

Cut me into pieces….
Still, calling your name….

Head to toe….
Dress like a lady….

Waiting for you….
My frozen Love….

With me or without me….
I'm not going anywhere….

A lady in her black & white memories….
Of her face against the World….

St. Mother

Cold-hearted killer….
You have been cursed….
For crucifying her mother….

St. Mother….
She must have suffered….
The unexplained pain….

In her name….
The Hapi Goddess soul….

Racism

Hoping to dilute the racism….
In the morning Sunrise….

And never come again….
The faded Moon again….

All light….
And bright….

Hope should grow….
And never fade again….

Melting Sky

Fire is melting the sky….
I am a little tipsy with shy….

Hold my hand….
Make me yours….
With pride….

Dewdrops

Sealed dewdrops….
Loving the fire inside my heart….

Shining like metal….
Shaping in and touched me….

Luster is sealed….
In my heart, beat….

I'm drenched with fire within….
The power of sealed dewdrops….

Heaven

Through eyes....
Traveling to heaven....

Through lips....
I am touching the morning Sun....

I'm your name....
You're my recognition....

Together....
We make fame....

Of World

Resting in my heart….
Pushing me hard….

The world is all grey….
And nothing last….

Not scared….
But the sound of me is trying to leave the past….

Still nothing left….
Dust of me might not last….

The Soul will be waiting….
In the green light grass….

Silly Solvent

Carbon blades….
I can tell you….
To use the good sign of oil or gas….

Melt in your self-control….
I will not give you any silly solvent….

Rose bright color….
Is to smile on your face….

Moist Color

Dissolve me in your inner circle….

You wear some dryness….

Moist color is about to drip in your arms around….

Nature

Sunlight makes me dark….

Superstorm is sandy in nature….

My life wants to sleep more….

In her natural, earthy ground….

Street Dog

What are you asking…?
You never lie to yourself….

True Human….
Friendly gesture….

Read my mind….
Love is all around….

Third Eye

Nights are blue....
Dark & Dim....

Life is going without any seem....

Soft-hearted you....
I'm a cruel third eye....

I'm your desire....
You're my self-shine....

Rimes

Welcome my rimes….
The golden glimpse….

Showering Sun….
In the morning whims….

Sweet outer….
Inner soft….

Melting Sun….
In the salty air….

Rimes rise….
Amplifying size….

Cover it….
Fine with the cloudy night….

My wristwatch….
In golden glimpse….

Next Height

The best night was all white….
You were having sweet sight….

Loving you was so easy….
Coming you is next height….

Will

Will power….
Can value our face & fate….

By searching life….
In this complex World….

One day….
This 'Will' give you your name….

In front of that Sunny day….
Quiet and It's whispering your name everyday….

'Will' give you the power to fight….
Again & again….
Don't know about you guys….
But my 'Will', will last forever….

I promise…!

Search your eyes and confined….
I'm brave…!

Can you tell me….
What you have done every day….
For surviving in this hell….

Because every day will make a difference….
How can you not interested to make a difference…?

Just because you haven't succeeded…!
Fight your war against your crime….
To be lazy and frighten….

Single days can make a difference….
Just leave your past….
And be in the present….

Will of desire….
Have the power….
In your head, don't get frightened with your mistakes….

Write now; you are trying….
One day you will survive all your fight with your smile….

One day you will have the story to tell….
Make mistakes and survive yourself….

'Will' is having the same effect….
Like in chessboard….
Standing last, but goes straight….

No fight….
Will is your mental game….

'Will' is not bound with time....
It can be created with time as strong as your mind....

Try me out....
Loud & Clear....
Saying it every day....

'Will power' is the only power....
That comes with you and last with you forever....

Sin

Nature couldn't be the reason....
Behind every natural calamity....

It's We, who have done the sin...!
By playing with her internal endure....

Nature is just telling us....
How to behave with her....

Her nature is to play with her beauty....
But don't take away her gentle beauty....

Her green essence....
Is dying with your nonsense...!